The Life of a Tree

written by **Island Lescure**
illustrated by **Marie Demont**

I start as a small seed fallen from a big tree.

Sometimes in a fruit,
sometimes in a cone.
Sometimes with many
and sometimes alone.

When the time and humidity are just right
I will send down a root
and then shoot up
into the light.

Then I'll grow as fast as can be
to reach the sky high above me.

As I grow into a mighty tree,
I'll make friends with those around me.
We'll protect each other from winds and from heat
by supporting each other where branch and root meet.

Underground we will trade
using connections we have made.
We'll do this in cahoots
with the fungi in our roots.

When all is right and well,
we'll make flowers with a sweet smell.
Then with wind, bugs and bees
we'll send pollen on to nearby trees.

At the end of this revelry
will be the start of a new journey.

New seeds will be born,
from which others will form.

As time goes by storms will come through
from which I will lose a branch or two.

But with this destruction
comes a new incarnation.
New cracks and hollows appear
for creatures from far and from near.

And after all this,
it is only a matter of time
before what is mine
becomes one
with others entwined.

I'll let go of the past

and move on at last.

Because at the end of the life of a mighty tree there'll be many new beings because of me.

Notes

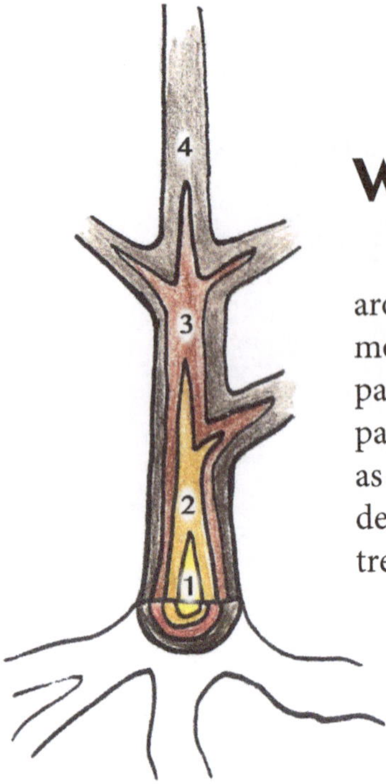

Wood rings - Page 6 -

Each growing season, when a tree grows, it puts on a new tree around and above the old one (this can be seen as "rings" in a log but is more like an envelope as it covers all parts of the tree). The outer, living part, grows and eventually the inner parts die. In some cases, the inner parts will be decomposed by fungi and bacteria to form hollows. As long as the tree can strengthen itself in time, hollows will not necessarily be detrimental to the tree. These hollows can provide new nutrients for the tree and habitats for other creatures.

Tree roots - Page 10 -

Contrary to what many people believe, a tree's roots do not mirror its above ground parts. The volume may be similar, but the structure differs; all parts of a tree need oxygen to live (to breath and use up sugars like us). Tree roots also need oxygen and can generally only obtain it in the soil near the ground level which is why most tree roots will only be found 60 centimetres underground. A tree's roots can generally extend up to two and a half times the height or canopy width of a tree.

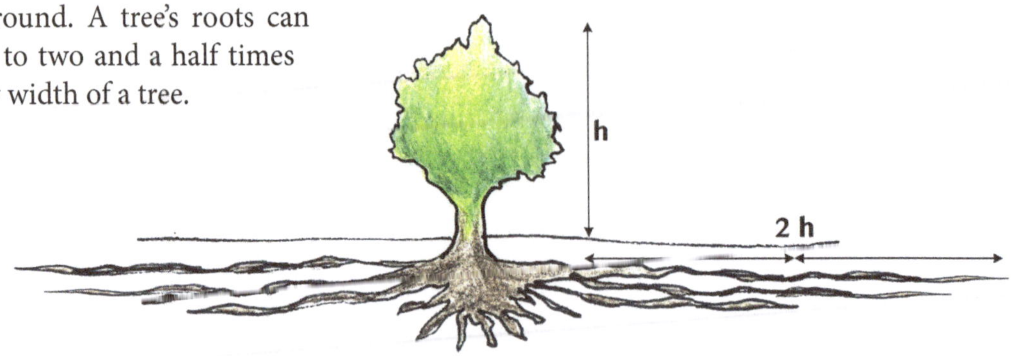

Support - Page 8 -

Trees support themselves and each other both directly (branch touching branch) or just by reducing wind speed to their neighbours. This can easily be seen when looking at the trees on the edge of a forest compared to the trees within; those at the edge will be sturdy and those within will be thinner and more fragile. The trees within don't need to grow as strong as they are protected from the others.

Fungi symbiosis - Page 10 -

Trees work with many fungi in symbiosis, where both benefit from the exchanges. Fungi get food (sugars) and the trees are better able to absorb water and some nutrients. There is a lot of evidence that shows that trees support other trees (of the same species or different ones) when connected by fungi hyphae.

Mushrooms - Pages 10, 18 -

Fungus fruiting bodies come in various forms such as mushrooms and brackets. They are like the flowers (reproductive bodies) of the fungi. If you see one (such as on a tree or around its base), you can be sure that its body is in the tree or beneath it. Some get very large. Some are beneficial to trees and others are actively pathogenic. Generally, if a tree is healthy, it can deal with having them around.

Honey fungus

Amanita muscaria

Chanterelle

Ganoderma

Life strategies - Page 23 -

Different trees have different strategies to deal with life and reproduction; some go for the long-term approach and others go for the grow fast, seed fast and die fast approach. And others go for everything in between. It is easier to observe a tree in different stages of its life when it is a long-term tree (though not by looking at only one particular tree as these can live hundreds or even thousands of years long). Long-term trees will concentrate on growing for a good third of their lives, then sustaining, defending and reproducing and finally declining and dying. These are all important parts of a tree's life.

First Published – 2020
by Island Lescure
Espace Auroville, Tamil Nadu India, 605101
island@treescapes.in

This edition - 2020

Printed at Repro India Ltd.